ISBN 978-1-5280-5460-7
PIBN 10047467

This book is a reproduction of an important historical work. Forgotten Books uses
state-of-the-art technology to digitally reconstruct the work, preserving the original format
whilst repairing imperfections present in the aged copy. In rare cases, an imperfection in
the original, such as a blemish or missing page, may be replicated in our edition. We do,
however, repair the vast majority of imperfections successfully; any imperfections that
remain are intentionally left to preserve the state of such historical works.

HISTORY OF THE GERMAN ELEMENT IN THE STATE OF COLORADO

A THESIS

PRESENTED TO THE FACULTY OF THE GRADUATE SCHOOL
OF CORNELL UNIVERSITY FOR THE DEGREE OF

DOCTOR OF PHILOSOPHY

BY

MILDRED SHERWOOD MacARTHUR

Reprinted from "Jahrbuch der Deutsch-Amerikanischen Historischen
Gesellschaft von Illinois," Jahrgang XVI, Chicago, 1917.

THE GERMAN ELEMENT
IN THE
STATE OF COLORADO

THE GERMAN ELEMENT IN THE STATE OF COLORADO.

ITS INFLUENCE ON THE ECONOMICAL, INTELLECTUAL AND SOCIAL DEVELOPMENT OF THE STATE.

By Mildred Sherwood MacArthur, Ph.D.

Wells College, Aurora, N. Y.

INTRODUCTION.

The plan of the present investigation, carried on during three years' residence in Colorado, and by a subsequent correspondence of fifteen months duration, embraces a brief historical sketch of the Germans in the State, an exposition of their services in representative pursuits and their share in developing the resources of the State, and a summary, with specific examples, of the influence of the German element on the religious, educational, political and social growth of Colorado.

The printed book was the least source of material. The Morgan Collection of Colorado books, begun in 1885, by Edward W. Morgan, consists of over 1,800 volumes, but it requires only a glance at the titles some of which are included in the bibliography given in this study, to be convinced that there is little of scientific value among them. Practically no attempt has been made to study the various national elements in the State. The 37th Anniversary edition (Jubiläums-Ausgabe) of the Colorado Herold published in 1907, contains an account of the Germans in Colorado and of various pioneer settlements, and a review of Colorado's industries.

The advantages and disadvantages attending research work in this vast field are readily apparent. An area of 100,-000 square miles, crossed by the main range of the Rocky Mountains, and having within its boundaries wide stretches inaccessible by any of the accustomed means of travel, present unusual geographical difficulties. However these are largely neutralized by the genial cordiality of the people of Colorado.

The student in the cause of research is aided by a keen spirit of progress, a desire to encourage and spread knowledge. This was the welcome met on every hand, in all classes of society and in all callings, from the Governor of the State to the worker in the mine whose accent told his German birth. Several pastors of German churches manifested a deep interest in this work and supplied valuable information. To many more people of Colorado I owe the facts made use of in this study, and incidents and examples from which I draw conclusions.

Information concerning the most distant sections came often from my immediate circle. From distant mining camps and from isolated ranches came interesting data through the courtesy of students attending the State University at Boulder. Records of the University show a large German-American element among the students from its earliest days. Not only was information derived from them directly, but interest in certain localities was aroused by them, compelling a visit. Thus I have visited Denver, Pueblo, Boulder, Colorado Springs, Colorado City, Manitou, Cripple Creek, Victor and many smaller towns. I have had several hundred personal interviews with German residents and others,—pioneers, statesmen, politicians, professional men, students, bankers, farmers, industrial workers and tradesmen; I have visited Germans in their homes, in their churches, and in their social activities. In this way I gained much valuable information and an insight into the atmosphere and setting of the German population, which alone makes possible an estimate of the subject of the influence of the German element in Colorado.

An extensive correspondence was another prolific source of information. In reply to my questionnaire addressed to the school superintendents of the sixty counties, I received answers from all but three. Of these one, Moffat county, was newly created and had, doubtless, no information to give; the other two were almost entirely Mexican in origin and interests. Whenever possible, I verified through direct communication all information derived from published sources.

THE GERMANS OF COLORADO.

The oldest file that has been preserved in the Denver Public Library of the first daily newspaper in Colorado, the "Rocky Mountain News" for 1864, furnished items concerning the Germans in Colorado twelve years before the Territory became a state. The daily issues of the German newspaper, "Der Colorado Herold", for the years 1910 and 1911 show the interest and activities of the Germans in the State at the present time. It is from all of these sources that the material for the following pages was derived.

Colorado is no exception to the rule that the far Western frontier has always been characterized by a predominance of the native American element in its population.[1] We are presented with the fact in the United States Census Report of 1910, that the Germans constitute 43% of the foreign population of the State. The geographical distribution is shown to be well balanced. The two largest cities, Denver and Pueblo, have respectively the largest and second largest German population in the State.

These statistics show that the German stock could not become as conspicuous in Colorado as, for example, in Wisconsin or Missouri, where the German element numbers in some localities one-third to one-half of the population, nor could their influence become as strong. But surpassing the proportion of their numbers the Germans in Colorado have become an important element in the development of the resources of the State, material as well as social and educational.

[1] The 13th Census Report (that for 1910) shows that but 16% of the total population of Colorado was of foreign birth. Other figures in this Census are:

MOUNTAIN DIVISION.

Total Population	2,633,517
German born	42,898
German parentage (one or both native)	92,070
Total Germans	134,968
Total foreign born	955,809

COLORADO.

Total Population	799,024
German born	17,071
German parentage (one or both native)	38,811
Total Germans	55,882
Total foreign born	129,587

CHAPTER I.

THE HISTORY OF COLORADO FROM THE EARLIEST TIMES.

INFLUENCE OF THE GERMANS ON EXPLORATION AND COLONIZATION.

It might seem a very simple matter to trace the history of a commonwealth that has not yet seen six decades pass since the period of its earliest settlement. But Colorado presents exceptional difficulties because of the loss of valuable records. The great fire of 1863 wiped out the whole business section of Denver, and the flooding of Cherry Creek during the spring of the same year, destroyed not only buildings, but valuable maps, papers, and court records. Thus the materials for the early history of the Commonwealth became very scant.

It was only a little more than one hundred years before Colorado became a state, that interest was first manifested in that section of the country. In July, 1776, two friars, Padre Silvestre Velez Escalante and Padre Atanacio Dominguez, undertook to explore a route from Santa Fe to California. To their efforts we owe much of our reliable information concerning the country at that time. In their descriptions they gave a glowing account of the grandeur of the forests and the beauty of the mountains and valleys, passing lightly over the roughness and impassibility of the country. Recent scholars deny the validity of all claims of exploration in Colorado previous to these of the latter half of the eighteenth century. They have also dispelled the once prevalent belief in the antiquity of the cliff dwellers, the ruins of whose civilization are still to be seen. To no distinct primitive race, but to the ancestors of the modern Pueblo Indians, are assigned the curiously inaccessible stone dwellings in canons and mesas.

The earliest authentic exploration in the Colorado territory took place in the period of the Spanish control. France had lost in 1762 the sovereignty over the tract west of the Mississippi known as Louisiana. In 1800 France regained and three years later sold this country to the United States. The

Louisiana purchase stimulated interest in the West. As a result, the expedition of Lieutenant Zebulon M. Pike was organized. Zealous explorers had other difficulties to overcome than those resulting from natural causes. A striking example of the discouraging effect of a single unfavorable report was the following. Major Stephen H. Long represented the region extending for a distance of five hundred miles east of the Rocky Mountains as unfit for cultivation and habitation. To this report Bancroft attributes the delay in securing it for the United States. Although such circumstances had a retarding effect on colonization, private expeditions of traders, forerunners of the great fur companies, advanced from time to time into Colorado. The first important forts within the present limits of the State were erected by the Bent brothers in 1832. During the years immediately following, numerous trading posts were established, among them were Vasquez's, Sarpy's, Fort Lancaster, Fort St. Vrain and El Pueblo.

Authorities assert that nothing of importance took place in Colorado between the year of Long's expedition (1819) and 1858. In the year 1842 government expeditions were sent out under John C. Fremont, but no important discoveries were made thereby.[1] Hard times following the panic of 1857, and discoveries of gold in California aroused interest in the far west. Tales of successful prospecting along the Platte river reached the ears of westward bound adventurers, not a few of whom paused for personal investigation. Some, on returning to the east, organized expeditions for prospecting in Colorado. Green Russell, a Georgian, was a member of one of these pioneer expeditions. Of the original company of 42 persons that set out in the spring of 1858, Russell with a half dozen men were the only ones with sufficient persistence to remain until a moderate degree of success met their efforts.

The political development of Colorado began at the time of these earliest settlements. In the autumn of 1858 a mass meeting was held in the settlement called Auraria, on which

[1] Charles Preuss, topographer, Fremont's assistant and companion, and Henry Brant, both of direct German descent, accompanied this expedition. Cf. Eugene Parsons, *The Making of Colorado*, pp. 88-116.

occasion Colorado was organized as Arapahoe County. A representative was sent from this meeting to the Governor of Kansas to secure the sanction of the Kansas Legislature to this action. In the same year the first of a long line of petitions to effect the erection of a separate government under the name of the Territory of Jefferson was sent to Washington. It was not, however, until February 28, 1861 that Congress passed a law giving to the land between the 37th and 41st parallels of north latitude, and the 25th and 32d meridians of west longitude the name of the Territory of Colorado. With this single creative act the Territory had for some time to be content. At this time, with the Civil War impending, national affairs were too engrossing. Washington itself was threatened: Congress was occupied with business less remote than that of the distant Territory. The recently appointed Governor, William Gilpin, received verbal instructions to exercise his own judgment and to do his best, for there was no time to attend to his affairs.

Constitution makers in Colorado had vast experience before they at last gained their purpose. A State Constitution was framed in 1860 but failed to receive the approval of the people. At the third session of the 37th Congress, 1862-63, a bill urging the passing of an enabling act, allowing Colorado to form a constitution, met with defeat. Congress granted this permission the following year but the constitution met the same fate as its predecessor. Finally a convention called in 1865 submitted a constitution that was adopted. This act was confirmed by Congress but was vetoed by President Johnson. Similar bills were revived and defeated periodically during the next decade. On March 3, 1875 an enabling act was passed, authorizing the electors to vote on the question of a constitution. The Constitutional Convention was held, and in the following July the new state was admitted to the Union. These, in brief, were the events attending Colorado's political struggle for being.

Many obstacles attended Colorado's rise to her present secure position. For many years this country was harassed by the powerful tribes of red men who dwelt within the territory. Treaties with the Ogalalah, Brulé Sioux, Arapahoes and Cheyennes are said to have existed as early as 1851. In 1862 the depredations of the Kiowas and Comanches were of such a nature as to demand military assistance. Some attribute this unrest of the Indians to the Civil War: Bancroft says that the savages did not choose to let the white men have a monopoly on fighting. An attitude of insolence became general, and in 1864 a combination was effected between the Sioux and the plains Indians with the purpose of driving out or exterminating the intruders—for such they regarded the white men. Outrages were committed and tales of repeated horrors were brought to the ears of the terrified citizens. Only a few miles from Denver a whole family was massacred. At this time the situation became very serious. Mail communication by the Overland Route was cut off. For a distance of 120 miles but one station on the route remained. The only connection with the rest of the world was by the ocean route to San Francisco. The red men continued their annoyances until forced to make peace by their too powerful foe.[1]

Indian wars were but one of the many discouraging elements to the early settlers of Colorado. In consequence of the drought of 1863 great numbers of stock perished. Fire worked havoc in Denver, destroying at one swoop $250,000 worth of buildings. But the trial was not yet hard enough: a winter of unusual severity followed drought and fire. With hay and grain at prohibitive prices and winter pasturage denied by climatic conditions, there was another tremendous cattle loss. The flood of the following spring was the final blow, though it proved to be the dark hour preceding the dawn. One million dollars worth of property was destroyed outright, farm lands were covered with a layer of sand and fruit trees were ruined. When we recall these almost insuperable difficulties and hardships, we are filled with all the greater admiration for the indomitable spirit of the pioneers.

The chief attracting power for Colorado has, until

[1] For an account of the German settlement at New Ulm, Minn., and the troubles with hostile Indians, see A. B. Faust, *German Element in the United States*, Vol. I, pp. 484-489.

recently, been her mineral wealth. Since coming into the dignity of statehood Colorado has seen two great "boom" periods. In the late seventies when gold digging was declining, a valuable discovery was made. The masses of carbonates that were cast aside by the seekers after the precious metal, were found to contain rich deposits of silver and lead. Soon the value of these metals increased many times, Immigrants poured into Leadville whose population in the first four months of the year 1879 grew at the rate of 1,000 a month; later this was tripled. The first smelter was completed here in 1878; by the end of the same year there were four others. In this beginning of the smelter industry two Germans were prominent,— Supt. Weise, of the original smelter, and A. Eilers who was owner of one of the first smelters in Leadville, and who later organized the Colorado Smelting Company at Pueblo.

A period of dullness in the years 1883-'85 was followed by a time of great prosperity. The advance of "dry farming," especially in Weld County, drew fresh flocks of immigrants. The year 1890 witnessed the founding of the richest gold camp in the world, at Cripple Creek, at which time was inaugurated the third great mining "boom". Having sketched briefly the history of Colorado from the time of its earliest exploration and settlement, let us examine the records to discover what part the Germans in the State took in these early developments.

The first city that was laid out and given a name in this new land was Montana, at the mouth of Dry Creek, six miles above the union of Cherry Creek and the Platte river. Later, the twenty blockhouses that constituted this settlement, were removed to Auraria, the first town of any importance in the region. In September 1858 St. Charles, the present site of East Denver, was incorporated. On November 17th it was reorganized and given the name of the former Governor of Kansas, John W. Denver. The claimants to the distinction of having built the first house in the new settlement were many. Philip Schweikert, of Columbus, Ohio, is said to have been one of the founders of Montana, and John J. Riethmann to have been the original builder in East Denver.[1] The latter was

---

[1] Hall, *History of Colorado*, Vol. I, pp. 181-82.

the eldest of four sons of Jacob Riethmann, a native of Canton Lausanne, Switzerland, who came to Colorado in 1859 and took a large tract of farm land about four miles from Denver. Through the provision entitling a settler who erected a house to thirteen lots, this enterprising family came into possession of forty odd lots which later became valuable property. These sturdy German pioneers were prominent both in industry and in financial fields. The elder brother, J. J. Riethmann, is said to have carried the first mail between Denver and Council Bluffs. He held also the position of first president of the German Bank.[1]

Another German who was well known as a progressive and philanthropic citizen, was Walter von Richthofen. By plotting and selling the suburban town Montclair, he had cleared a fortune, and then planned to furnish the people of the vicinity with a park for public pleasure. He had erected a castle in splendid German style and was engaged on the work of laying out the park, when the scheme was checked by his death.[2] Johan Ernst Madlung, a native of Reichenbach, Saxony, was one of the first settlers in the town of Harman, in whose growth and incorporation he took an active interest.[3] Another "first settler" was Charles Mater, a native of Cassel. He started the first building on the original town site of Leadville in June 1877. The grocery store which he opened, was a very successful establishment and became the headquarters of the town.[4]

Custer County became the seat of one of the most important, though shortlived German colonies in the State. The leaders, Carl Wulsten, Theodore Hamlin and Rudolph Jeske, impelled by a desire to ameliorate the unfavorable conditions

[1] *History of Denver*, pp. 556-571. A brother, Emile, for several years Swiss consul for Colorado, filled various political offices,—representative to State conventions, county commissioner, etc. In the latter capacity, he secured for his locality excellent road and bridge facilities. Two other brothers, Frederick and Louis, and two sisters, Mrs. John Milheim and Mrs. Foreman, came also to Denver.

[2] Hall, III, p. 285.

[3] *Denver and Vicinity*, p. 607.

[4] Fossett, *Colorado*, p. 410; Kent, *Leadville*, pp. 130-131.

of Germans working in Chicago, selected a colony site at the extreme southern end of the Wet Mt. Valley in December 1869. Early the following spring the colony, consisting of 65 families, (in all 367 persons) arrived and established the town named Colfax. Many reasons have been advanced to account for the early collapse of the colony, which lasted but six months. According to one authority, the colonists, being accustomed to city life, found themselves at a loss here and proved ungrateful.[1] Another says: "Lack of religious and social principles, and absence of military discipline left the colony to fall to pieces from inherent weakness."[2] At any rate the benefit aimed at is generally conceded to have been achieved independently of organization. Some took land claims, which subsequently became very productive. Others removed to different parts of the Territory, but all are said to have remained in it.

The earliest settlements in Saguache County were made by German pioneers. In 1865, a number of Germans, members of Company 1, 1st Colorado Volunteers, among whom were Captain Charles Kerber (Körper), Lieutenant Walters, and George Neidhardt, settled at Kerber Creek. Peter Luengen, a native of Rhine Prussia, was one of the earliest

[1] Bancroft, p. 595; Hall, Vol. I, p. 542.

[2] *History of the Arkansas Valley*, p. 694.
Soon after his arrival, Wulsten was made Brigadier General of the State Militia. He is the man to whom the community, and especially Custer County, owes more than it will ever repay. Through his tireless energy, he became one of the wealthiest citizens of the county. His reputation as man, miner, mine manager and engineer is an enviable one. It is said that his maps of mining properties may still be found in New York mining offices. Early in his experience in the colony (1871) his opinions concerning the mineral wealth of the region were published in the *Pueblo Chieftain*. These predictions have been tested by time and proved reliable. Concerning the Chicago Colony, the report was spread broadcast that it was an attempt on the part of the government to reclaim southern Colorado from democratic folly, which attempt, if successful, would be repeated in the San Luis Valley and elsewhere. Then when Colorado should become a state, the Republican party would be assured of its support. What truth, if any, was attached to this rumor is not known.
Another native German among the creators of Custer County was the Hon. Charles Sieber, a native of Neissen in Prussian Silesia. He was State Representative in the first session of the Legislature.
—*History of Custer County*, 694ff

pioneers in the country. He is still fond of relating his early experiences. One of his narratives shows why the German pioneer was often through diplomacy able to win out when others, with less tactful methods, failed. While crossing the plains, Mr. Luengen encountered on the North Platte a band of Indians, 52 in number. As was customary on such occasions, a conference preceded any action on either side. During this interview, Mr. Luengen sat enthroned on his horse and won the hearts of the red men by trading with them for their buckskins. In exchange for a skin he dealt out a cup of flour and a slice of bacon, and gave evidence of the shrewdness necessary for business success.

With few exceptions the Germans in Colorado came as individuals rather than in colonies, and the instances are very rare where they clung together clannishly. This fact indicates the possibility of ready assimilation that the American nation delights in seeing in her immigrants. What the influence of the German pioneers in Colorado would have been had a more clannish spirit existed, no one can say. But what the Germans there have done in braving the terrors of the frontier, in producing order out of chaos, in developing material resources and in planting the institutions of a higher civilization in the new land can be learned from specific instances, selected here and there from the mass of material obtainable. The Germans in Colorado furnish an example of the typical German characteristics, long-suffering endurance, patient plodding, strict business integrity, respect for law and order, keen initiative in agricultural and commercial lines, accurate training and efficiency both in the foregoing and in professional fields, a sense of the importance of recreative enjoyment and a fine show of public spirit in the advancement of philanthropic and educational projects. These were far from being the qualities that characterized their forerunners, the early trappers and traders. The task of these later comers, the German pioneers, was a difficult one. Henceforth thrift, economy and industry were to be in the lists with utter improvidence, wastefulness and sloth. Randall Parrish describes the easy access into a western community in these words: "The West asked no question of any man; all that he had been in other days, east of the Missouri, was blotted out. Here he stood eye to eye with his fellows, and no voice challenged him." [1]

To review the facts gained in this brief historical outline of the colonization of Colorado we found first that the year 1859, perhaps the most interesting in the history of settlement in Colorado, brought several influencial Germans to this frontier community. The original builder in East Denver, and one of the founders of Montana were both Germans, John J. Riethmann and Philip Schweikert, respectively. The pioneer work of von Richthofen as public benefactor was noted. Carl Wulsten, another of Colorado's progressive German pioneers, was the founder of the Chicago Colony. At the organization of the Pioneers' Association (June 22, 1866) which was to include only settlers of the years 1858-'59, there were present Andrew Sagendorf, John J. Riethmann and George Schleier. In various sections of the state Germans were among the earliest settlers. The first permanent settlers in Castle Rock, Douglas County, where now fully 75% of the population is said to be German, were Jacob Bower, and the two brothers Benedict and Jacob Schultz. In Buena Vista, Chaffee County, a native German, Gustav Krause, started a pioneer tent-grocery.[3] Fremont County has always had prominent Germans among its residents. Of them we call attention to the following pioneers: William Kroenig, George R. Schaffer, August Heckscher, Mark Schaffenburg, Charles Boettcher, Frank P. Schaeffer, Michael Dueber, Rudolph Jeske, Augustus Sartor, Julius Ruf, and Albert Walter.[4] In Park County too, we learn of many German settlers. Jefferson County is proud to recall among its prominent residents the following native Germans: Adolph Coors, a Prussian by birth, Joachim Binder, born in Wittenberg, Peter Christensen, a native of Schleswig, Adam Oehus, a native of Hesse-Cassel, Adam C. Schock, a Bavarian,

---

[1] Randall Parrish, *The Great Plains*, pp. 337, 340.

[2] Hall, I., p. 396.

[3] *History of Chaffee County*, pp. 477-543.

[4] *History of the Arkansas Valley* (Fremont County), pp. 543-689.

and Henry F. Wulff, born in Schleswig-Holstein.[1] Elbert County had among its German settlers August H. Beuck, a native of Kiel, Holstein, who, in his adopted country became a prominent ranch man.[2] Another successful German rancher was Henry Gebhard, a native of Baden.[3] Other Germans of note in Elbert County are Anton Schindelholtz, J. George Benkelman, J. J. Kruse and John Hoffman.[4] Prominent Germans in Gilpin County are Jacob Kruse, mayor of Central City, 1874-'76, the Kountze brothers, bankers, Judge Silas B. Hahn, Charles Weitfle, photographer, Henry Altvater, Theodore Becker, Andrew Bitzenhofer, Maxwell Bolsinger, Henry Bolsinger.[5] A progressive farmer of Larimer County, John Hahn, was also a native German. Another German, Samuel Clammer, wins words of the highest approval from his historian.[6] Some of these men will receive more detailed mention later in this paper, but, in a list of the Germans who aided in the pioneer work of settlement, they could not be omitted.

CHAPTER II.

THE INFLUENCE OF THE GERMANS IN COLORADO ON THE DEVELOPMENT OF THE MATERIAL RESOURCES:—MINING AGRICULTURE AND INDUSTRIES.

With much of the West still unpopulated in the middle of the 19th century, there was needed an especial attraction to draw colonization to one section more than to another. This attraction, and a very sensational one in the case of Colorado,

[1] *History of the Clear Creek Valley*, pp. 558-599.

[2] *Denver and Vicinity*, p. 266.

[3] *Denver and Vicinity*, p. 378.

[4] Supra, 519, 625.

[5] Hall, III, p. 408.

[6] Watrous, *History of Larimer County*, pp. 364-365.
Other Germans in the vicinity are Rudolph Boeram, Dr. Schofield, Dr. Moench, Chris Molly, Watson Ziegler, Rev. Burghardt, Louis Wetzler, Frank Wicks, Peter Kern, Peter Scheldt, Vincent Demmel, John L. Herzinger, August Rohling, and Emil Loescher.

was furnished by the tales of unprecedented wealth to be found in her gold mines. Gold mining, or indeed, mining of any sort, did not long retain its popularity in the Centennial State, but to it belongs the credit of having served as the initial stimulus to immigration. The history of mining in Colorado, pictorially represented, would resemble the main range of the Rocky Mountains that extends north and south through the State, with three great elevations separated by depressions. The elevations, or "boom" periods represent the Pikes Peak "gold fever" of 1859, the silver discoveries in Leadville in the late '70's, and the almost unparalleled gold discoveries in Cripple Creek in 1890. When one studies the thrilling accounts of mining in Colorado with a desire to learn what connection the Germans in the State have had with this industry, two closely related facts come to light. First, many Germans who were intimately involved in the mining interests in Colorado, advanced during their connection with these interests, the cause for which they strove, and won thereby fame and wealth. Secondly, the cases are rare in which the Germans remained for a long time in this pursuit. This fact is easily explained. Mining is the most fascinating and perhaps the most tragic game of chance, absolutely incompatible with the typical German characteristic, thrift. When the German miner made his little "pile", he invested it straightway in a safer and steadier enterprise and turned to a profession or to a pursuit adapted to a life of peace and contentment. Shrewdness and perseverance are native German qualities which are of inestimable service in mining ventures. There are, in mining deals, many illustrations of the one characteristic without the other,—of dogged determination with no foundation on which to rest, and again, of shrewdness so calculating that it never ventures,—but it is the happy blending of the two that seems to produce the best results.

A sufficient number of Germans have engaged and are still engaged in mining in Colorado, so that a history of her mining industry becomes also a page in the history of the German element. The thrilling tales of adventure that make up the story of the mining "booms", as well as the tragic despair that followed not only in the times of general depression, but also upon individual failure, are too well known to require repetition here. A recital of the accomplishment of German miners in Colorado would prove almost as familiar a tale, but a roll-call of some of the more significant names is highly desirable, that we may see how large a part the Germans have taken in developing this important resource. A veritable king among miners was a native of Minden, Prussia, August Rische, by name, who came to Colorado during the first decade of the mining excitement (in 1868) and made the valuable discoveries that founded his wealth.[1] Another native German who won distinction in mining circles, was Charles A. Martine, who began his mining operations in Colorado by opening an assay office in Central City in 1866. Impelled by the silver excitement, he removed the following spring to Georgetown where he made the pioneer demonstration of ore sampling and stamping in Colorado. To him belongs the credit of being the first man in the State to manufacture silver bars, as well as being the original shipper of ores from Clear Creek County.[2] Philip Mixsell, of German parentage, erected the first custom stamp mill in Idaho Springs, owned several large mines and was proprietor of the Mixsell Tunnel, formerly the largest project of the kind in the State.[3] The famous Prussian Mine in the Gold Hill district was discovered in April 1861 by George Zweck, a native German who, recognizing at once the value of the ore, carried out his project of developing the mine though it was at great personal sacrifice.[4] A noteworthy example of a German who was attracted to this country by the tales of mineral wealth, but who did not long continue in the pursuit of mining interests, was Charles Mater, a native of Cassel.

[1] Kent, *Leadville*, p. 127; *History of the Arkansas Valley*, 207-388. Mr. Rische discovered valuable fissure veins at the head of the Arkansas, also the "Little Pittsburgh." Owned large interests in the New York Mine and in the San Juan and Rico districts.

[2] *Denver and Vicinity*, p. 479; *History of Clear Creek and Boulder Valleys*, pp. 521-522.

[3] *Denver and Vicinity*, p. 419.

[4] Bancroft, Vol. XXV, p. 649, footnote.

His long and active life in Colorado to which he came in 1860, was devoted to mercantile pursuits and to civic interests.[1]

We may conclude this brief sketch[2] of Colorado Germans in mining ventures with a typical tale of the hardships endured by the men who came as pioneers to the west in quest of gold. Charles Lerchen, a pioneer of 1859, was a member of a party of four that set out from Davenport, Iowa, to investigate the celebrated gold country. While on their journey they were met by men returning discouraged from the very land to which they were going. Their unfavorable reports disheartened Mr. Lerchen's companions, who decided to abandon their mission. At Fort Kearney they deserted the more persistent German, leaving him, as his only assets besides his indomitable will and courage, a yoke of oxen and a sack of flour. He joined forces with another company which also turned back within 200 miles from the goal. Finally after a trip of 90 days, Mr. Lerchen reached Denver, alone.[3]

As before said, Colorado began its career as a mining State. The gold seekers came with no other thought than to make their fortunes and then return to "the States". But many of the pioneers of 1859-1860, failing in their mining ventures, turned their attention to the cultivation of the soil. Before 1870 when the Greeley Colony attacked the problem in earnest, agriculture in Colorado was a primitive kind. The average rainfall of eastern Colorado is estimated at 6-15 in. per annum. This arid region was indeed, in early days, considered a desert, unfit for the home of civilized man. Some

[1] *History of the Arkansas Valley*, pp. 207-368.

[2] Others who deserve mention here are John Zinsendorf, E. H. Gruber, Caspar S. Desch, Henry Kneisel, Christian Manhart, Fred Buckman, William Tick, John C. Kaufman, C. C. Miller, Joseph S. Beaman, Andrew Bitzenhofer, Barnard Schwartz, Samuel Neuhaus, Frederick Kohler, Henry Neikirk and Erl von Buddenbrock. Of these all but two, whose parents were Germans, were native Germans.

[3] Cf. *Denver and Vicinity*, p. 635. Mr. Lerchen was born near Dresden in 1839. He at first engaged in mining in the Blue river country. At various times he was occupied with copper and silver lode mining in Custer and Huerfano Counties, and himself discovered several gold mines. In less than three years he had left mining for other pursuits.

of the pioneers were familiar with artificial irrigation as it was carried on in California and in the Rio Grande valley of New Mexico. They made attempts at a similar sort of irrigation along Clear Creek, the Platte river and Boulder Creek and thereby established the fact that the soil was fertile and would under proper conditions, produce with abundance. Even as late as 1874 it was believed that the uplands were incapable of cultivation, but when it was discovered that the soil of the bluffs was as rich and as productive as the lower land, changes in the manner of ditch construction took place. It was then that the big canal corporations came into existence. The construction of great irrigation canals in northern Colorado, in the San Luis Valley and in the valleys of the Arkansas and the Grande rivers brought water to thousands of acres thus opening the land to settlement. The advantages of irrigation farming are everywhere recognized. The increased production soon replaces the original outlay for canals and water works. The increased gain both in quantity and quality of produce is causing Colorado to forge ahead as a farming State.[1]

The men who were active in organizing companies for the construction and maintenance of irrigation systems in Colorado, laid the foundation for her agricultural career. In the front rank of these pioneers were many German citizens. Chief among them were George Stearly and Andrew Kluver who were instrumental in constructing the canals of the Water Supply and Storage Company, one of the largest and most important irrigation systems in northern Colorado.[2] Others who have taken active part in construction and management of irrigation systems are David Birkle, Fritz Niemeyer, Alex-

[1] At present water rights go generally with the land at the time of its purchase, which, when unirrigated, is of little value. Private companies build storage reservoirs and canals to convey the water from them or from streams to the land to be irrigated, the main canals being tapped by many laterals. From each lateral small ditches are dug with scraper and plough to carry the water to the various fields. Colorado farmers began early to show their pride in raising produce of unusual excellence. *The Rocky Mountain News* of September 3, 1864, tells of the remarkable stalk of yellow corn bearing six large, full grown, perfectly formed ears, that was brought to Denver by A. Sagendorf from a farm 11 miles up the Platte.

[2] Cf. Watrous, *History of Larimer County*, pp. 482, 484.

ander Milheim, Andrew Hagus, John H. Behrens, Joseph C. Cramer and Ernst von Buddenbrock. Five of these men have filled the office of president of various ditch Companies, Kluver, president of the Water Supply and Storage Company, Birkle of the Meadow Island Ditch Company, and also of the Beaman Ditch Company, Andrew Hagus of the Fulton Ditch Company, and Ernst von Buddenbrock of the Model Land and Irrigation Company. The latter company, one of the late constructions, reclaimed 20,000 acres of desert land. Other important offices such as treasurer and superintendent have been filled by some of the above mentioned Germans, and all of them have been actively engaged in the promotion of artificial irrigation in Colorado.

Once given a fertile soil, perhaps the foremost condition for success in agriculture is a taste for, or even better, a scientific knowledge of soil tilling. Many adventurous pioneers, lured by the generous distribution of homestead land, failed or met with but meager success in agriculture, because they knew no more about it than they did about prospecting, and in farming chance played a smaller part. The German pioneer, however, peculiarly adapted to agriculture from long and thorough acquaintance with it, almost invariably succeeded. The Germans too, possessed the desirable characteristics of steady plodding industry and persistent effort. Many of the wealth seekers had imagined Colorado to be an enchanted land, the very sands to contain shining gold, the streets to be paved with silver and the bushes to yield treasure. Such, naturally, were disappointed at the grim reality. Whether or not the Germans shared this belief, they did not give up in despair when its falsity was established. The adventurous spirit of the west seems to have infused a little of its dash into the native Teutonic apathy. The same disposition that we saw was so successful in the pursuit of mining, willingness to take a good risk, mingled with a great deal of caution, met with an equal degree of good fortune here.

The industry in which Colorado leads all States is sugar beet culture. This has been a wonderful incentive to colonization and to the development of the State; it has suggested to other lines of agriculture its own intensive methods and it has brought about many of the great irrigation projects. Sugar factories have been established at Eaton, Greeley, Loveland, New Windsor, Longmont, Fort Collins, Sterling, Brush, Fort Morgan, along the Arkansas valley at Rocky Ford, Lamar, Las Animas, Holly, Swink and Sugar City, and along the Grand river at Grand Junction, Monte Vista and Delta. These factories are reported to be successful, and they are aiding the various commercial, manufacturing and agricultural industries of the State. The development of this industry has, in a few years, built railroads, towns and irrigation works. Population and wealth have increased rapidly and capital has been attracted toward building up the enterprises that make for the greatness of a State.[1] In many of the districts where the great sugar beet fields are under cultivation, Germans are prominent among the workers. The people accustomed to similar employment in Europe seem to have responded to the call for laborers here. Many of them, especially in Larimer and in Delta county, are Russo-Germans, that is, Germans who formed colonies in Russia under very favorable conditions made by that government which subsequently were endangered. Peculiarly fitted for this work, thrifty and economical as they are, these recent arrivals have met with great success.[2]

[1] Cf. *Colorado State Board of Immigration*, pp. 10-13. For dairying, truck gardening, poultry and bee keeping, etc., see p. 13 ff.

[2] Peter the Great offered privileges to German colonies in Russia,— among them, exemption from taxation and from military service for a term of years. In 1783 Catherine II imposed a poll tax on the peasants in the Baltic provinces in order to prevent their developing in a way that would bring about estrangement from Russia. She was too wise and liberal not to see that the independent German culture of the Baltic provinces was far ahead of the rest of Russia, and instead of becoming a menace might serve as a model.—Dr. Otto Hoetzsch, Professor in the Royal Academy, Posen. Cambridge, *Modern History*, Vol. VI, p. 694. It seems very probable that the ancestors of the Russo-Germans in Colorado might have been among the emigrants from West Prussia, the foundation stone of whose colonization was the manifest of the Russian empress, Catherine II, July 22, 1763. This promised unhindered immigration privileges to all foreigners in Russia; choice of home in city or country; to poor families, assistance with travelling expenses and liberal aid from the State treasury by the erection of factories; freedom from taxes for some time; especially, complete religious freedom and the right to settle in groups on their own strips of land, to

They find it possible to live at about the minimum cost; they are all, including the women, accustomed to field work, and by the combined efforts of steady industry and strict economy they are rapidly gaining comfortable competencies, and in a small way, becoming landed proprietors. They manifest an ambition to rise from the state of mere hirelings; their interest in their adopted land is strong enough to cause them to desire to remain in it. As they are, in many cases, still ignorant of the English language, they are very clannish in religious and social life. They are rated among the best workers, and set a high standard of efficiency, thus producing among the other inhabitants a sentiment favorable toward their nationality.[1]

A few examples of typical German farmers in Colorado will serve as reminders of the kind found here, while a catalogue of names of others recall many who have assisted in developing the State. A prominent farmer, a Prussian by birth, Frederick Gross, had, previous to his departure for the new country, mastered at home the art of intensive farming. This knowledge, together with his energy and industry, enabled him to outstrip his neighbors in annual yields. He soon became known as "the farmer who never failed to raise a good crop." He gradually made purchases of land and added thereto improvements until he ranked as one of the foremost men in his vicinity.[2] Another example of the success that follows

---

build churches and schools, to appoint their own pastors, and to have the inner management of such colonization in the hands of their own officials. Such colonies were to be free from military service and to enjoy the favor of the government. These colonists were, in religion, Mennonites. In view of the military developments of West European peoples at the end of the 18th century, it was becoming more and more difficult for these people to retain their peculiar position in the State (their religion forbade them to bear arms). Russia had, however, great territories along the Black Sea in which she wished to replace the nomads of Mongolian blood living there, by people experienced in tilling the soil, and many German colonists settled there, with exemption from military service. In the age of universal military service this privilege was in danger of being abolished, owing to the jealousy of less fortunate neighbors, and emigration of German Mennonites from Russia to the United States began. Cf. Wedel, III, p. 120 ff.

[1] "Kleine Gruppen suchten auch in Colorado fortzukommen," we read in Wedel, IV, p. 191.

[2] Cf. *History of Larimer County*, p. 485.

unremitting labor, is furnished by the experiences of Andrew Hagus, a German pioneer of 1859. After a few months' trial at mining he started an entirely new product in this region. He began to raise vegetables to supply miners and had splendid results in this much needed line. He introduced on his farm the first mowing machine, rake, etc., ever seen in the county (Arapahoe). His brother, John G. Hagus, who followed him in 1860 to Colorado, illustrates by his success the power of energy and determination.[1]

A very close relationship exists between forestry and irrigation. The establishment of forest reservations has been largely in the interest of agriculture and irrigation. Although the science of forestry is still new in this country, Colorado is fortunate in having one well trained forester among her pioneers. He was a native German, Frederick J. Ebert, who came to Denver with an engineering corps from St. Joseph, Missouri, and made the first survey west of the Missouri river. As he was aware of the advantages of forestry laws and regulations, he was eager at the very opening of the country, to encourage necessary legislation. Truck and landscape gardening have always been largely in the control of the Germans in Colorado.[2] In this calling they have furnished very creditable results. As early as 1869, George Neare, popularly called "Dutch George," was a truck gardener at the mouth of Lone Pine Creek.[3] Peter Fischer, a native of Nassau, was a pioneer nurseryman on Cherry Creek, about one and one-half miles from Denver.[4]

Fruit growing, now the leading industry in several large districts of Colorado, was, a few years ago, believed to be impossible. Now, the names of Delta County, the San Luis Valley and Rocky Ford are celebrated, far and wide, for ex-

[1] *Denver and Vicinity*, 246 ff.; Hall, IV, 484. At the New York Land Show, November 1911, the two prize winners for the best exhibits of sugar beets were Coloradoans. One of them was V. Deich of Julesburg.

[2] Cf. Denver Real Estate and Stock Exchange, *Annual Report*, 1891-'92.

[3] Cf. *History of Larimer County*, p. 193. Mr. Neare removed later to Elkhorn Creek where, in 1871, he was killed by a bear.

[4] Cf. *History of Clear Creek and Boulder Valleys*, p. 564.

tensive fruit culture. Colorado is now entitled to fame as a horticultural State. The leading fruit raising counties of the northern part of the State are Boulder, Jefferson and Larimer. The Arkansas Valley, with its center in Canon City, is probably the site of the first successful orchards in Colorado. The valleys of the Grande, the Uncompahgre and the Gunnison and, on the western slope, Montrose, Delta, Mesa and Garfield Counties are all important fruit raising sections.[1] The first fruit orchard in the Mountains is said to have been planted by a native German, Louis Wetzler, who came to Greeley in 1871. He was at first subjected to the scorn of his neighbors, who declared his undertaking an impossibility. Later, he was able to prove that they were wrong. By his example he encouraged many others to follow in this pursuit.[2] Another native German who disproved the theory that fruit could not be successfully grown in Colorado was John G. Bader, a pioneer farmer on Left Hand Creek in Boulder County.[3] Albert G. Snyder, a native of Canton Berne, met with very favorable results with his large orchards, also his crops of grapes, strawberries and blackberries.[4] John D. Stickfort, a native of Hanover, planted on a very uninviting tract of wild prairie land in Jefferson County in 1882, an apple orchard which was said to be the best producer in the county. In 1897, Mr. Stickfort gathered from it more than 1,000 barrels of apples.[5] In 1859, William Hoehne came to Las Animas County where he was the first farmer settler and one of the most enterprising of the German pioneers. He is credited with having built the first mill, with having introduced the first threshing machine and with having started the cultivation of strawberries, apples, cherries, etc., in the county. He conducted his farming in a progressive fashion. For example, he conceived the idea of planting crabapples and cottonwood trees in alternate rows, thus affording wind breaks

[1] Cf. *Jubiläums-Ausgabe des Colorado Herold*, p. 45.

[2] *History of Larimer County*, pp. 416-417.

[3] Cf. *History of Boulder Valley*, p. 611.

[4] Cf. *Denver and Vicinity*, p. 750.

[5] Cf. Supra, p. 1024.

and timber protection. For several years, he operated 1,000 acres of land on which he raised splendid crops.[1] Among the many other successful fruit growers and gardeners among the German settlers in Colorado we would mention especially Frederick C. Schroeder in the Clear Creek Valley, and Frank W. Ricks in the Little Thompson Valley.[2]

Although Colorado was long famed for its cattle ranges, it took considerable time for the stockmen to discover that they could increase their profits enormously by employing other methods than, as formerly, shipping the cattle to eastern markets.[3] Among men who were not content to follow the beaten track, were several alert German citizens who turned their attention to the dairy industry. Prominent among them were George Rittmayer, Johann Madlung, Emile Riethmann, Frederick Affolter, Charles Bangert, T. U. Bausinger, William Bramkamp, Ferdinand Ebert, Eugene Farny, P. W. Snyder, Jacob Wolfensberger, all of whom were native Germans with the exception of Mr. Snyder who was of German ancestry, and Messrs. Riethmann and Wolfenberger who were both born in Switzerland.[4]

The Denver Stock Exchange was first organized in 1887, but the pioneers had made small but successful beginnings with the cattle business previous to that time. Especially in the beet raising districts, sheep raising is of importance. The two are supplementary as the beet tops and pulp have proven to be the best diet for the animals, thus providing a use for the waste product. The sheep industry is said to have produced the greatest clear profits of any of Colorado's agricultural

[1] Cf. Hall, IV, p. 194.

[2] Cf. *Denver and Vicinity*, pp. 1024; *History of Larimer County*, pp. 383-384.
Gustav Hermanhofer, Park Superintendent of Pueblo, had set out in City Park 400 various plants (according to the *Colorado Herold* for February 27, 1912), in order to establish the fact that they will grow in akaline soil.

[3] In this connection, cf. F. L. Paxson, "The Cow Country," in the *American Historical Review*, Vol. XXII, No. 1 (October, 1916).

[4] Cf. *Denver and Vicinity*, pp. 598, 725, 879, 995, 1089; Hall, IV, 396ff.

THE GERMANS OF COLORADO.

industries. Among the early pioneers who carried on an extensive business in this line was a man of German descent, Ernest Bartels.[1] A native German pioneer of 1860, Jacob Scherer who was born near the city of Dresden, was one of the early cattle men who from humble beginnings achieved great wealth. Unless a cattleman had control of great capital he had to be content to isolate himself and to "rough it". There was, however, a way for a man with persistence to build up a fortune. The big drivers who had in their care 800 to 1,000 head of cattle, had no time to care for the sick cattle or for the calves that were born on the way. Thus the man who was willing to submit to personal sacrifice and hardship, could follow the trail from Texas to Montana and pick up these unfortunates and with them form the nucleus of a profitable business. Charles Lerchen, another native German, carried on a stock ranch in Arapahoe County as early as 1868. He is said to have brought into the State more finely bred bulls than any other man, and he is the first man in the State to give premiums for prize cattle. John Walters, later head of one of the largest firms in Denver and one of the largest sheep raisers and dealers in the West, laid the foundation for his business by purchasing several hundred head of sheep in New Mexico and driving them to the Denver market. His interests extended later to sheep breeding and raising in Wyoming, also to buying and ranging in Utah, Colorado, Kansas and Nebraska. He was a member of the Standard Meat and Live Stock Association of which another native German, Frank X. Aicher, was also a member.[2] Jacob Scherrer, a stock man since 1868, was at one time owner of the Denver Stock Yards, the first establishment for supplying the beef market of the city.[3] August Beuck, whose native city was Kiel in Holstein, was owner of 1,000 acres of land in Elbert County and also of nearly as many head of cattle, and was a member of the Colo-

[1] Cf. Hall, IV, pp. 333-337.

[2] Cf. *Denver and Vicinity*, p. 726. Mr. Walter's father was born in Würtemberg.

[3] *History of Denver*, pp. 601-602. Mr. Scherrer of German and French descent.

rado Cattle Growers' Association.[1] Another German member
of this Association was Henry Gebhard, who after spending
ten years in Elbert County buying, selling and shipping cattle,
became a member of the Burghardt Packing Company and
later organized the Colorado Packing and Provision Company,
the largest packers of beef and pork in the State. To its
founder is attributed the prosperity of the organization.
Anton Schindelholz and John G. Benkelman are also on the
roll of members of the Colorado Packing and Provision Company. Elijah Bosserman is general manager of the Denver
Live Stock Commission Company, which he organized in 1886.
This was the first company to locate at the Union Stock Yards
in Denver. Jacob Schütz whose tract of 2,500 acres of land
in Douglas County was in 1860 a wild, unimproved claim, by
his strenuous efforts adapted the same to his purposes and
made a great success with raising thoroughbred, shorthorn
cattle.[2] In the instances cited above, we again see many Germans taking the lead in an important agricultural industry.

Many of the successful farmers in Colorado, and among
them are Germans, have achieved their prosperity through a
kind of farming elsewhere unknown, the so-called "dry
farming". It seems logical that the land that produces wild

---

[1] Cf. *Denver and Vicinity*, p. 226. Mr. Beuck was one of the first
stockmen to dehorn cattle.

[2] Cf. *Denver and Vicinity*, pp. 332, 378, 425, 519, 923. Also, for
Benkelman, *History of Denver*, p. 332.

Among other stockmen, "old-timers," deserving of their success and
among the most substantial and most highly respected citizens of their
respective communities was John Hahn, for thirteen years stock raiser in
Larimer County. Mr. Hahn, a German by birth (see Supra, 933, and
History of Larimer County, 391), acquired by his judgment and energy
1,240 acres of excellent land. Here also we mention John L. Mitch,
of Prussian parentage, part owner of 3,500 head of sheep in Bent
County; Ludwig Kramer, a native of Wittenberg; William Barth, a
native German, president and organizer of the Denver-Texas Cattle
Company; Charles Snyder, whose father was a native of Canton Berne;
Ferdinand Ebert, George C. Fahrion, Andrew Hagus, Christian Kill-
kopf, J. E. Madlung, George Stearly, and Lewis Hagus, all of German
birth, and Rudolph Koenig, born in Switzerland, and Frederick Schroeder and Michael Leuhart, of German descent. For detailed accounts
of the above see *Denver and Vicinity*, pp. 208ff., 768, 773, 786; *History
of the Arkansas Valley*, pp. 765-889; Hall, IV, 449-450, 484, 494, 529,
503; *History of Larimer County*, pp. 476, 484.

the cactus and sage brush should yield valuable agricultural products. The secret, in this arid country, lies in producing a soil that hinders the moisture from being absorbed by the hot, dry air. In order to make the lower layer of soil as yielding as possible to a large water content, the surface is kept finely pulverized but firm and compact. The Colorado "dry farmers" have accomplished the remarkable results that a rainfall of 12 inches can be so conserved that it yields better effects than are attained in regions where the average moisture is 24 inches. Ten thousand square miles of desert land where only cactus, sage brush, sunflowers and prairie grass once grew, are, as a result, now yielding rich harvests of wheat, corn and clover. To this branch of agricultural industry the German farmer has adapted himself readily. He realizes that tireless industry is the price set upon a good harvest and he pays this price willingly. We cite here only a few of the many instances that show how the German immigrant by persistent efforts, strict economy and shrewdness has made for himself a solid place.

The case of Andrew C. Kluver is typical. When he came to Fort Collins at the age of 25, he put to immediate use his only capital,—a span of horses, a wagon and cash amounting to $31. He occupied himself, at first, with odd jobs of teaming; later, he ran a threshing machine and baler. In less than two years after his arrival he was owner of three teams which he traded for a small stock of groceries, engaging then in the mercantile business. His success was remarkable. He became owner of a good farm in the Cache La Poudre Valley, of the Craddock ranch at Livermore, and of a well stocked cattle ranch on Rabbitt and Meadow Creeks. He acquired as well, large interests in financial organizations,—in banking and in the Water Storage and Supply Company.[1] Another native German, Lewis Schroers, who settled on a farm on the Platte River near Island Station in 1860, since then so improved his land that it became one of the finest farms in the county. He is described as possessing "the usual steady, persevering energy

[1] Cf. *History of Larimer County*, p. 398.

characteristic of the Germans."[1] Anton Schindelholtz came to Colorado in 1860 with no capital save physical strength, steady determination and thrifty habits. It did not take him long to discover that his dream of gaining sudden wealth was an idle one. Sober judgment gaining the mastery over his enthusiastic visions, he bought a ranch, stocked it with cattle and conducted a successful dairy, becoming thereby a man of wealth and position.[2] Another tale of "Poverty to Prosperity" is illustrated in the experiences of Emile Riethmann, a pioneer of 1859, whose history has already been considered in the pages treating of the German pioneers in Colorado. The oft repeated assertion that prosperity seems to have followed the Germans, is unconsciously explained by those who testify: "There are few shiftless ones among the Germans."

Native Germans and their sons have engaged in nearly, if not indeed all the industries that flourish in Colorado. The brewing and bottling business is practically monopolized by them. Prominent names in this industry which has, in Colorado, ranked high, are Coors, Endlich, Frederick, Fuelscher, Burghardt, Neef, Lammers, Suess and Zang, all of whom with but a single exception are of German birth. Philip Zang who was born in Bavaria in 1826, arrived in Denver in 1869, where he entered the employ of John Good as superintendent of the latter's brewery. In July 1871 he purchased the Rocky Mountain Brewery, the pioneer establishment in Denver, which later was said to be the largest brewery between St. Louis and San Francisco.[3] Adolph Herman Joseph Coors was born at Barmen, Rhine Prussia, February 4, 1847. He went to America in 1868, to Denver in April 1872. In June of the same year he started a bottling business with John Staderman. In October 1872, in company with Jacob Schueler, he established a brewery in Golden. He later purchased his partner's interest in the brewery which became one of the

---

[1] Cf. *History of Denver*, p. 587.

[2] Cf. *Denver and Vicinity*, p. 519.

[3] Cf. *History of Denver*, p. 651; Hall, IV, p. 631; *Denver and Vicinity*, 5496. See also *Jubiläums-Ausgabe des Colorado Herold*, p. 60.

largest and best equipped in the State. Agencies have been established at Denver, Pueblo, Trinidad, Colorado Springs, Aspen, Fort Collins, Louisville, Blackhawk, Como, Meeker, Buena Vista, Del Notre, Creede, Gunnison, and Aquilar.[1]

German bakers enjoy wide fame and Colorado does not detract therefrom. Starting with the earliest times, when in 1859 Henry Reitze opened the first bakery in Denver and offered to accept gold dust in exchange for his products,[2] and going to the time when Otto P. Baur became owner of one of the city's largest candy establishments which still bears his name, there have been many Germans in Colorado prominent as bakers and confectioners.[3] Among the pioneer German bakers were Hans J. Kruse, Adolph Schinner, J. J. Riethmann, and Albin Maul.

Hotel keeping has been a close second to brewing with the Germans in Colorado as far as popularity and success are concerned. Charles Eyser, a native of Holstein, was in the early 60's proprietor of the "German House" in Denver.[4] Another native German, Otto Kappler, has held the position of manager of both the Metropole and the Brown Palace, one of Denver's finest hotels.[5] Other Germans prominent as hotel owners and keepers are John Zimmermann, Frederick Christman, E. Menig, Charles F. Hertel, Conrad Frankle and Charles Nachtrieb. Zimmerman, a native Swiss, founded a celebrated mountain resort when, in 1880, he constructed a few rough cottages near his sawmill. As the resort became popular, the commodious hotel, the Keystone, was erected. Christman was the founder of a favorite road house in Virginia Dale in Larimer County. Menig was a successful hotel keeper in Denver in the early days, being connected with the Fremont

[1] Biographical material furnished by a member of the Coors family.

[2] This distinction is disputed by the bakery of J. J. Riethmann and John Milheim, pioneers of 1859. Cf. *History of Denver*, p. 518.

[3] Cf. *Denver and Vicinity*, p. 637. Mr. Baur was born in Würtemberg.

[4] Cf. *History of Denver*, p. 426.

[5] Cf. Hall, IV, p. 492.

House and later with the Milwaukee House, which he built, and conducted until 1889. Hertel came to Colorado in 1860 and had many thrilling encounters on the frontier with hostile Indians, in which he proved himself a man of valor as well as of enterprise. Frankle who constructed the Washington Hotel on 5th Street in Denver, and Nachtrieb, the builder of an excellent hotel at Northrop Station, Chaffee County, were both successful German hotel keepers.[1]

Several German families in Colorado have made a signal success along mercantile lines. Pioneers among them were the three Bartels brothers, Louis, Gustave and Julius, natives of a small town near Göttingen. The former came with his original stock of merchandise in the summer of 1861, crossing the plains with an ox team. Nine years later he and his brothers were successfully conducting the houses they had established at Pueblo, West Las Animas, Walsenburg and San Antonio.[2] William and Moritz Barth, who were born in Dietz, Nassau, were pioneer shoe manufacturers and wholesale dealers in Colorado, whence they too came in 1861.[3] August and Philip Rohling, two brothers from Dielingen in Westphalia, conducted large stores in Blackhawk and in Fort Collins.[4] Edward Monash, another native German started in 1866 the first department store in Denver, "The Fair", where, by his energy and good judgment, he built up a profitable business.[5] Other prominent pioneer merchants among the German residents of Colorado are George Tritch who first offered for sale a varied assortment of farm implements;[6]

[1] For details of the above, see *History of Larimer County*, pp. 370, 466; *Denver and Vicinity*, p. 486; *History of Denver*, 426; Hall, IV, 530, 600; *History of the Arkansas Valley*, pp. 477-543.

[2] Cf. Byers, *Encyclopedia of Biography*, p. 343; *History of Denver*, 329.

[3] Cf. *Denver and Vicinity*, pp. 205-208ff.

[4] Cf. Supra, pp. 399, 977; *History of Larimer County*, p. 392.

[5] Monash was born in Posen. Cf. *Denver and Vicinity*, p. 369.

[6] Tritsch was born in Baden. Cf. *History of Denver*, pp. 612-613.

John J. Lindner, plumbing and hardware merchant;[1] Samuel Strousse, Hyman Schradsky and Julius Berry, clothing dealers;[2] Gustav Krause,[3] Adolph Brocker,[4] grocers; Herman H. Cordes, carpet dealer;[5] Ignatz Haberl, jeweler and lapidary;[6] Henry P. Nagel and J. J. Hense, both jewelers in the 60's.[7] Another pioneer merchant of 1864 whose advertisement shows how infused he was with the spirit of the west, was George Teiklar. He claims the following: "I will furnish my customers with every variety of meats from a mutton chop to an ox".

The name of Maximilian Kuner, the "grand old man of the business world of Denver", stands very near the head of the manufacturing industry in this locality. His genius for organizing is responsible for the Colorado Manufacturers' Association, established in 1906, an association for mutual assistance and protection to the shippers of the State.[8] His brother, J. C. Kuner, who preceded him to Colorado, started the Denver Pickle Works in 1872. From a very small beginning,—Mr. Kuner at first did his own "teaming" in a wheelbarrow,—the company of which Mr. Kuner is president has grown to such proportions that it is reported to supply the

[1] Father was a native of Würtemberg. Cf. *Denver and Vicinity,* pp. 1080-1081.

[2] All three native Germans. Cf. Supra, pp. 1104-1105; *History of Arkansas Valley,* pp. 765-825; Hall, IV, p. 581.

[3] Krause was born in Germany. Cf. *History of Arkansas Valley,* pp. 477-543.

[4] Brocker was born in Prussia. Cf. *History of Denver,* p. 349.

[5] Cordes born in Bremen. Cf. Supra, p. 376.

[6] Haberl born in Hanau, near Frankfort on Main. Cf. Byers' *Biography,* p. 444.

[7] Nagel born in Schleswig-Holstein. Cf. *History of Denver,* p. 537. Among the hundreds of successful German merchants in Colorado are I. H. Kastor, Edward Kerstens, F. L. Rohlfing, George Hamburger, Albert Abel, Fred Mueller, Maximilian Spanier and George Reinhardt. For above see *Rocky Mountain News* for 1864.

[8] Born in Lindau, Bavaria. Cf. *Sketches of Colorado,* 1911, pp. 256-2557. *History of Denver,* p. 490. Data also from residents of Brighton.

trade in all the western States. The main factory is located in Denver, branches existing at Brighton, Platteville and Greeley, on which hundreds are dependent for support. Charles Boettcher, a Prussian by birth, was a leading promoter of the Colorado Sugar Manufacturing Company of Grand Junction, and was one of the builders of the first sugar beet factory in Colorado.[1] In Loveland he built another plant similar to the one in Grand Junction. This factory is the property of the Great Western Sugar Company of which Dr. Franz Murke, another native Prussian, is chief consulting chemist. The celebrated "Blackhawk" wagon which has won a reputation throughout the country, was invented by William Tick, a native of Stargard, Pommerania, and sprang from the need of a better equipment for hauling ore and for general mountain service.[2]

Attempting to fill long-felt wants many of Colorado's German pioneers have advanced the progress of the community by inventions. August Pirch, a native of Prussia, was one of · these men. He invented a "Sulky Ditching and Sidehill Plow", an ingenious contrivance incorporating several new features, and also a tool called the "Improved Blacksmith Wagonmaking combined machine", an article adaptable for the operation of hammer, shears, reciprocating saw, drill, punch, chisel, etc.[3] The names of Robert Bandhauer and Henry F. Meine, both native Germans, are familiar in Denver, both men being distinguished for splendid mechanical skill and for ingenious inventive power. The latter, a skilled cabinet maker, invented and patented a combination billiard and game table.[4] A German who has resided in Denver since 1880, Jacob Fitting, established in 1892 the Pioneer Iron and Wire Works. Today his business is said to rank among the greatest of its kind in

[1] Cf. *Sketches of Colorado*, p. 150.

[2] Cf. *Denver and Vicinity*, p. 1024.

[3] Cf. *History of Denver*, p. 548.

[4] Cf. Supra, pp. 342, 518-519.

the west.[1] His is the distinction of introducing the first wire fence manufactured in Colorado. Adolph Rauh, a Bavarian, engaged on coming to Denver in 1870, in the marble cutting business with F. R. Trotzscher. A year later he constructed a steam saw mill in West Denver. He expended large sums in the search for stone quarries and was successful in locating the first in the State, among them the famous Castle Rock Quarry and those at Canon City and Pueblo. He is entitled to credit for having established the first steam marble works in Denver.[2]

John J. Bitter came to Denver in 1879 and five years later started his business as contractor[3] and builder. It is of interest to note that the first bridge constructed in the Colorado Territory was ascribed to George C. Schleier, a native of Baden. On his way to the Gregory Gold mines he was checked near Golden by high water in Clear Creek over which he erected a bridge at a cost of $600. Mr. Schleier is said also, to have erected one of the first two-story buildings in the State. In the severe winter of 1858-'59 he hauled timber for the purpose a distance of 25 miles.[4] A German woman, Mrs. F. C. Bray, formerly Miss Agnes Braum who was born in Berlin, is a capable member of the Laundrymen's Association. She has proved herself an efficient business woman in the laundries which she successfully conducts.[5]

The German element in Denver has aided the city's development through the active part taken by its representatives in real estate interests. Among the early members of the Denver Real Estate and Stock Exchange were Walter von Richthofen, H. C. Mentzer, Max Baer, Niesz & Company and

[1] Mr. Fitting was born in Westhofen. Cf. *Jubiläums-Ausgabe,* p. 46.

[2] Cf. *History of Denver,* p. 562.

[3] Father of Mr. Bitter was a native of Oldenburg. Cf. *Denver and Vicinity,* p. 511.

[4] Cf. *History of Denver,* p. 605-606.

[5] Cf. *Denver and Vicinity,* p. 567. For many other instances cf. *History of Denver,* pp. 450, 533, 630-631; Hall, IV, pp. 434-435, 475.

G. O. Shafer.[1] Alfred H. Gutheil, a native German, bought
and plotted the Gutheil Gardens in 1889. Seven years later,
the Gutheil Park Investment Company organized with Mr.
Gutheil as president and general manager.[2] Another section
of Denver bearing the name of the German settler who pre-
empted it originally, is Wagner's Addition, named for Herman
Wagner.[3] Some of Denver's finest building sites were com-
prised in the section of land, or "Addition", named for Adolph
Schinner, a native German who, in 1860, came to Colorado on
horseback.[4] W. H. Buchtel, son-in-law of the celebrated P. T.
Barnum, for whom he named the town which he laid out, has
been a strong factor in developing Denver real estate.[5] Peter
J. Frederick, whose parents were native Germans, held at the
time of his death the following offices: Vice-president Zang
Realty and Investment Company, Welton Street Investment
Company, St. James Investment Company, German-American
Trust Company and Lakeside Realty and Amusement Company.[6] E. H. Asmussen, a native German, and John Milheim,
a Swiss, have engaged with success in real estate ventures in
Denver.[7] As a real estate undertaking of quite a different sort
we recall the amusement resort at Lindenmeier Lake, whose
originator was William Lindenmeier, Jr., of German descent.[8]

The actual beginning of the smelting industry in Colorado
was made at Malta in 1877 when August R. Meyer erected in
California gulch a small smelter to reduce ores. As he was
in need of lead ores the following winter, he experimented
with the mineral on the dump of the Rock mine and found the
result very satisfactory. Later the smelting industry attained

[1] Cf. *Denver Illustrated*, p. 38.

[2] Cf. *Denver and Vicinity*, p. 258.

[3] Cf. Hall, IV, p. 623.

[4] Cf. *History of Denver*, pp. 594-595.

[5] Cf. *Denver and Vicinity*, p. 297.

[6] Cf. *Sketches of Colorado*, p. 409.

[7] Cf. *History of Denver*, p. 518; Hall, IV, p. 366.

[8] Cf. *History of Larimer County*, pp. 281-282.

to great proportions in that part of the Arkansas Valley.[1] Frank Guiterman, a German of the second generation, holds the highest position in his line in the United States. He is General Manager for the American Smelting and Refining Company, Colorado Department.[2] Rudolph Koenig, a native German, pioneer of 1867, was for nine years President and General Manager of the Gold Smelting Company.[3] A. Eilers, a prominent native German in the smelting industry in Pueblo, first became identified with that industry in Colorado, when in 1879 he erected a smelter in Leadville. Later he organized the Colorado Smelting Works at Pueblo.[4]

On a slightly different level from the preceding stands banking, a business which suggests always that the persons participating in it inspire an unusual feeling of trust. In the early days, when financial institutions in Denver were purely personal ventures, Charles and Luther Kountze, two of the four sons of Christian Kountze, a native of Saxony, organized and successfully operated a banking house in that city. This became later the Colorado National Bank whose president and cashier respectively, were Luther and Charles B. Kountze. The latter, at the time of his death, November 18, 1911, was reported to be the wealthiest man in the State.[5] The German Bank, later incorporated as The German National, was organized in 1874 with J. J. Riethmann, George Tritch, C. A. Fischer, L. F. Bartels, J. M. Eckhart and Conrad Walbrach among its officers and directors.[6] Mr. Bartels was also active in promoting the Colorado Savings Building and Loan Asso-

[1] Cf. Hall, IV, p. 431.

[2] Cf. *Sketches of Colorado,* 1911, p. 165.

[3] Cf. *Denver and Vicinity,* p. 809.

[4] Mr. Eilers was born in Germany and educated at the Mining School at Claustal and at Göttingen. Cf. *Who's Who in America!*

[5] Cf. *Rocky Mountain News,* August 25, 1864. The Rocky Mountain National Bank was established by the Kountze Brothers in Central City in 1866. Of C. B. Kountze, the *Boulder Herald* for November 18, 1911, said: "The career of C. B. Kountze in large part is the history of Denver, the story of Colorado."

[6] Cf. Hall, II, pp. 210-211; III, pp. 198-202.

ciation, whose purpose is to aid the poorer classes in erecting homes.[1] The German-American Trust Company, established in 1906, is one of the large and flourishing banking houses in Denver at the present time. Its President, Godfrey Schirmer, and Cashier Dieter are much respected German citizens who have made their way through difficulties from small beginnings. Mr. Schirmer was honored a few years ago by the Order of the Crown, 4th Class, conferred by the Kaiser. The two brothers, William and Moritz Barth, were prominent in the City National Bank of Denver, the former as vice-president, the latter as director.[2] In the Bank of San Juan and Del Norte, they were both directors and stockholders. Frederick J. Ebert, a prominent German pioneer who has been mentioned in other connections, was stockholder, director and, at one time, president of the Exchange Bank.[3] From the annual statements given out by the banks of Denver, in December, 1911, it is easy to see what a large proportion of bank officials are at the present German either by birth or by extraction.[4]

Summarizing what has been told in the preceding sketch of the men of German blood in Colorado's industrial life and their influence on the development of her material resources, let us recall the prominence of these citizens in the mining industry. Although, as we have noted, this is a hazardous pursuit unsuited to characteristically German qualities, the Germans in Colorado have been fairly well represented as pioneers, as promoters and as successful constructors of mines. And aside from the part they have played in developing the mineral resources of the State, they have exerted an influence

[1] Cf. Byers, *Encyclopedia of Biography*, p. 343; *History of Denver*, 329.

[2] Cf. *History of Denver*, pp. 342-343, 345.

[3] Cf. *History of Denver*, pp. 416-418; *Denver and Vicinity*, p. 400.

[4] In the above mentioned list occurred the following names: John E. Hesse, F. A. Eickhoff, B. F. Salzer, H. M. Hubert, Dr. Charles Jaeger, Otto Sauer, Henry Gebhard, Thomas S. Hayden, Meyer Friedman, E. S. Kassler, August Schmidt, J. C. Burger, E. J. Weckbach, G. M. Hauk, G. B. Berger, Harold Kountze, William B. Berger, J. H. Kolb, A. J. Bromfield, Luther M. Beck, William F. Huffman and Ernest R. Stadler.

needed here, perhaps, more than elsewhere. Teutonic calm, sometimes miscalled "stolidity", often produces order in chaotic situations and saves the venture from ruin. Again, as we turn to the agricultural industry, the close and prosperous rival of mining in Colorado, we find a great predominance of Germans among the leaders. In irrigation projects, in general and truck farming, in cattle raising, sugar beet culture, fruit growing, forestry and in the comparatively new line of dry farming, Germans have excelled. Finally, in practically all of the State's industries are to be found representatives of the German element. Especially prominent in brewing, bottling, baking and hotel keeping, they are also at the fore in mercantile lines, in the manufacture of farming implements, wagons, etc., and in smelting. We have also seen them filling important positions of trust in financial circles and promoting real estate projects.

CHAPTER III.

THE INFLUENCE OF THE GERMANS IN COLORADO ON THE RELIGIOUS, EDUCATIONAL, POLITICAL AND SOCIAL DEVELOPMENT OF THE STATE.

From the very beginning of settlement in Colorado the Germans, individually or in groups, have been working for the betterment of the community. Hand in hand with the development of the material resources that we have studied in the preceding chapter, has come branching along cultural lines. Colorado has just passed the fortieth anniversary of its statehood but, as a whole, it bears little resemblance to a pioneer State. Its citizens have been ready to work for its intellectual and social growth and, from the first, Germans have been prominent in educational, professional and philanthropic undertakings. The church and the school have about equal claim to precedence in the field, and both have played an important part in the education of the people. The first year of important colonization in the Territory, 1859, saw the Rev. J. H. Kehler, of direct German descent, conducting the first Episcopal church in the region, St. John's in the Wilderness.

He was for several years pastor of this church, which he him-self established. He served also, as Chaplain of the First Colo-rado Cavalry, accompanying them on the campaign against the Texas rangers. In 1873 the first German church was erected in Denver. At present there are in that city nine churches whose services are conducted in the German language. Throughout the cities and towns of the State German churches appear in numbers corresponding to the population.[1] In the beautiful Montezuma valley, in the southern part of the State, are two German colonies that bear a marked religious char-acter. The Lutheran settlement is at Thompson Park, about 20 miles from Durango, and at the other end of the valley, about 7 miles from Dolores, is the so-called "German" settle-ment, Catholic in faith. No one can follow the press notices of the social and religious services of the German churches in Colorado without being aware of the flourishing condition of these organizations. We make no claim for the service of the German church in Colorado in influencing the religious development of the community other than that rendered by every prosperous church or religious organization, but we do hold that the German church has had a powerful cultural effect in that region in that it has kept alive in its worshippers the language of their fathers. In many cases, the church pro-vides the only opportunity to the younger generation for prae-ticing the German language. On their neighbors, the zeal with which the German citizens strive to preserve their native

---

[1] Denver has 3 Evangelical, 2 Methodist, 1 Presbyterian, 1 Congre-gational, 1 Baptist and 1 Catholic church in which the German language is used. Pueblo has 1 German Lutheran, 1 German Methodist and 1 German Catholic church. There are in Colorado over twenty places where services are conducted under the government of the German Lutheran Synod. Berthoud has a German Congregational church. Fort Collins has a thriving German Evangelical congregation. The pastor, Rev. Paul Burghardt, conducts services also in the Christ Con-gregational church (German) at Wellington. This is one of four churches in the town which is an important shipping point. Loveland, with a total of 16 churches, has 5 German organizations. (See *History of Larimer County*, pp. 198, 207, 211, 259.) The Society of Seventh Day Adventists have 4 German churches in Colorado, located at Brighton, Hygiene, La Salle and Loveland. H. A. Aufderhar, a member of the executive committee of the Seventh Day Adventist Association of Colo-rado, has charge of the work among the Germans.

tongue, produces a deep effect, and in them is aroused an interest in this language. An understanding and appreciation of a people whose customs differ from our own has a broadening influence. No doubt the tolerant attitude for which the west is celebrated, is due to the existence of many national stocks in an environment whose tradition has been neighborly cooperation and social equality.

As we examine the field of education, we see that the Germans on the frontier lost none of their native desire for it. Even when their means were very limited, they contributed generously to the maintenance of schools. In the fall of 1859, the same year that the Mission church was established by the Rev. Kehler, F. B. Steinberger started a little school in Denver with but 14 pupils. Amos Steck was another German citizen who was early identified with educational work in Denver. One of the two men to whom is ascribed the successful establishment of the Denver School system and its subsequent management is Frederick J. Ebert, a German prominent also as engineer and surveyor. Among other important positions, Mr. Ebert was at one time President of the Board of Regents of the State University, of which Board he was for years a member. Other German citizens who in official positions on school boards have promoted the cause of education in their communities, are Eugene Farny, an Alsatian by birth, Peter Theobaldi, a native of Bavaria, William H. Meyer, John H. Behrens, Jacob Schütz, George Tritch, Max. Herman, Oscar J. Pfeiffer and others.[1]

From the very earliest days, Germans have played an important part in making and improving journalistic opportunities in Denver and in the other cities of the State. The founder of Denver's oldest newspaper, the "Rocky Mountain News," the first daily issue of which appeared August 18, 1860, was the Hon. Wm. N. Byers, a German of the second generation. As manager and editor Mr. Byers did much to attract settlers to Colorado by publishing articles explaining the

[1] The report of the secondary schools in Colorado for 1912 as to the Modern Foreign Languages taught gives the following: 98⅜% of the schools offer German, 12% French and 15% Spanish.

resources of the State, the advantages for stockraising and farming, the mineral wealth and the fine climate. The early files of this paper are one of the best sources for a history of Colorado. The general tone of the earliest issues of the daily is progressive. With daring and breadth of thought, improvements are suggested in civic life and subjects foreign to the average pioneer are discussed. From the continual reference to the Germans and to things pertaining to the Germans, it is evident that these subjects were expected to interest a large class of readers.[1] A lively editorial entitled "The Value of Amusements" says: "It is impossible to suppose that a human being can labor exclusively. He must be amused, he must laugh, sing, dance, eat, drink and be merry." [2] This sentiment, precisely opposite to that of the early American colonists, was that preached and put into practice by the Germans. They were the hardest workers and probably the most habitual players in whatever community they were found. Among the pioneer settlers of the west they instilled the principle of the blessedness of innocent enjoyment. Among other German pioneers who were effective journalists in the employ of American newspapers in Colorado was Herman Beckurts who in 1875 purchased the "Denver Tribune", said to be the leading

[1] An editorial of November 17, 1864, has the following: " 'Ausgespielt'—this Teutonic synonym for 'played out' is very expressive when pronounced with the broad German accent." "What do you mean by Teutonic as you apply it in your items occasionally?" is quoted January 14, 1865, and, after an excellent analysis of the word, he sums up: "Teutonic, therefore, may mean an intelligent German, a flaxen-headed Hollander, a lager-loving Dutchman, a persevering Prussian or a peddling Pole." A news item, August 5, 1865, says: "The Germans do not have the words 'churchyard' and 'burying ground' to designate their places of interment; they use the beautiful and suggestive expressions 'God's Acre' and 'Court of Peace'." The editor calls Denver "a bookless burg" and, after giving his readers a severe rating for their remissness, he makes many practical suggestions for improving conditions.

[2] In announcing the performance of "The Robbers," February 1, 1865, he says: "The author of the 'Robbers', which will be performed tonight, was J. C. F. Schiller, a great German poet, dramatist and historian." Following this was an excellent biographical sketch of Germany's beloved poet. The educational character of many of the short items is evident. For example, there are articles on "The Drama," "War in Ancient Times"; he encourages reading of good books, and expresses a desire for a public library.

paper between the Pacific and St. Louis. As a result of his efforts at reconstruction, the paper quadrupled its circulation in three years.[1] Frank Kratzer and John P. Heisler were for twelve years newsgatherer and editor respectively of the Daily Herald.[2]

The *37th Jubiläums-Ausgabe des Colorado Herold,* published in 1907, furnishes a complete survey of German journalism in Colorado. The first number of the first German newspaper in the State, *Die deutsche Presse des grossen Westens* appeared July 16, 1870. Its short life of but three months is attributed to the lack of business qualities in the genial editor, Augustin Knofloch, and in no way to the Germans of the State, whose enthusiasm was great. Early in the summer of 1871 appeared *Die Deutsche Zeitung,* edited by Frank Kratzer, but before spring this, like its predecessor, had passed away. The fatal blow was struck, it is thought, by the business depression under which Denver was at the time suffering. On May 4, 1872, William Witteborg edited the first number of the *Colorado Journal.* Like its predecessors, it appeared once a week, the first two numbers in editions of 3,000 copies each. The paper received hearty support from the increasing German population throughout the west, the editor possessing the desirable requisites for making his undertaking a success.[3] The paper went into the control of a corporation, of which Mr. Witteborg retained control until 1879, when both the daily and

---

[1] Born in Brunswick. Cf. *History of Denver,* pp. 313-314.

[2] Cf. Hall, IV, pp. 472-473, 490-491.

[3] Born at Soest, Westphalia. Cf. *History of Denver,* p. 635.— Meanwhile there were numerous unsuccessful attempts to found a second German newspaper. Some ended in failure, others became fused into the *Colorado Journal.* There is record of the following: *Colorado Courier,* 1873; *Colorado Post,* 1879; *Sonntagspost,* 1880; *Colorado Staats-Zeitung,* 1882; *Denver Herold, Denver Fidibus,* 1883; the *Denver Herold* and *Denver Fidibus* became united under the name *Fidibus-Herold.* In Leadville, during the "boom" period, a German newspaper made its appearance. For some time Pueblo supported the *Pueblo Anzeiger,* but it was finally superseded by the *Colorado Herold* and the *Denver Herold.* In the middle of the '90's, during the silver agitation, several numbers of the *Silberglocken,* an eight-page weekly in quarto form, appeared. The *Harugari Ordensblatt,* 1896, gave rise to the weekly, the *Colorado Vorwärts.*

weekly were turned over to Wyl von Wymetal. He, in turn, was succeeded by Roesch and Company in 1883, subsequently by Kratzer and Reinhold, who retained the management until 1893, when it was assumed by R. Walter from whom it passed into the hands of the German Publishing Company.

We can get some information concerning the service rendered by the paper in a study of its columns. The purpose of the paper as stated in its anniversary edition, is "Pflege der deutschen Sprache, Sitten und Gebräuche". This purpose seems to be in the mind of the editor throughout, in advertisements as well as in the editorials. The former, by furthering the interests of both subscribers and supporters, serves the community, and the editorials are typical examples of the courage of conviction. By granting them press notices, the *Colorado Herold* aids and encourages all the German interests, commercial, political, religious, educational and social. The paper exerts a linguistic influence in that it is expressed in comparatively good German, which it keeps alive in the community. In its four page supplement which is issued each Saturday, there appear stories, short scientific articles and long novels in serial form.

With music everywhere in the United States guided so generally by German residents, it were idle to add long lists of the people who, in Colorado, support and in many cases furnish the music. One public-spirited German citizen of Denver, Mr. Fritz Thies, who is accorded universal praise for his generosity and zeal in securing the best music for his city, must be mentioned. It means more to a pioneer community, which the west still remains in matters of the fine arts, to get the rarest musical treats, than an outsider can imagine. Scattered here and there throughout the State one finds often in the most unlooked for spots, Germans disseminating their music and encouraging a taste for this and other fine arts.[1]

[1] A typical case was that of a German mining expert, Mantius by name, who in the barren mining community of Georgetown, during the silver excitement, made his humble home an attractive center for those of the pioneers who enjoyed music. He was himself a good musician. There are many instances of prosperous German music masters in Colorado.

Both the German and American newspapers give prominent mention to the organized life of the German societies in Colorado. Of these there are more than a score in Denver alone,[1] some of them beneficial in character, all of them encouraging the perpetuation of interest in the particular section of the fatherland from which their adherents came. This may be seen from their entertainments. For example, the *Schwäbischer Unterstützungsverein* on the occasion of its Silver Jubilee, March 10, 1912, presented in Suabian dialect, a peasant wedding ceremony. Masked balls, with prize awards for the best Swiss costumes, are a favorite form of entertainment with the *Schweizer Maennerchor*. The *Denver News* of January 12, 1912 published an illustrated account of the 25th Anniversary of the Bavarian Society. In the chorus of 125 male voices that furnished part of the entertainment, were several who had participated in the Passion Play at Oberammergau, one of the performers, indeed, being related to John Lang, the *Christus* in the play. The *Edelweiss*, dainty flower of the Alps, was imported for decoration and for souvenirs on this occasion. Not alone from their nature and development, but from their very ideals, the *Turnvereine* are separated from the other societies. The latter are organized chiefly for the promotion of local or social interests, but the *Turnverein* stands for the education of the masses, and forms an important factor in the progress of American civilization. The Germans themselves give the following estimate of its value (cf. *Colorado Herold*, May 3, 1912): "Von allen Gütern, welche der deutsche Einwanderer von seiner alten Heimat nach den Gestaden Amerikas gebracht, ist das edelste und bedeutendste die deutsche Turnerei". That this society was in a flourishing condition as early as 1870, we learn from the "Colorado

---

[1] Denver has the following benevolent and social organizations conducted wholly or in part by the Germans: Alsace-Lorraine; Badischer Unterstützungsverein; Bavarian Verein; Bavarian Verein, Ladies' Section; Colorado Lutheran Men's League; Colorado Pioneers; Deutsch-Amerikanischer Unterstützungsverein; East Denver Turnverein; Schweizer Männerchor; Socialer Turnverein; West Denver Turnverein; there are nine lodges of the Deutscher Orden der Harugari; five lodges of the Orden der Hermanns-Söhne; also the German Krieger-Verein. Cf. *Denver Directory*, 1912.

Gazetteer", a publication that appeared in that year, and which gives the following: "This German society, so well known and so much revered by the children of the Fatherland in every country, has already been firmly established in the principal cities of the Territory".

The principal *Turnvereine* of Colorado are the East Denver, the West Denver and the Social Turnverein, all three in the capitol city, the Leadville and Grand Junction Turnverein. Formerly societies existed at Central City, Pueblo, Cheyenne, and Albuquerque. As early as 1862, the East Denver organization was firmly established. The regular schedule of these societies perpetuates a live interest in the members themselves. The daily announcements in the German newspaper under the heading, "Heutige Versammlungen" serve as a guide to the life and activities of the Germans in Denver and vicinity.[1] The character of the social evenings of the *Turnvereine* is such as to stimulate regular attendance. The reports of new members admitted at each meeting indicate a steady growth. The influence of these societies is that they have given encouragement and instruction in athletics, thus developing the idea of producing a sound body in which the mind will the better dwell, and teaching the value of healthful exercise not only as a health preserver but as a means of wholesome enjoyment. They were in the field before the Young Men's Christian Associations, on whom they have exerted a helpful influence. They have supplied instructors for these

[1] The National *Bundesfest* was held in Denver in the summer of 1913. Preparatory to it the three societies of Denver held a great "Schauturnen" in the Auditorium on May 3, 1912. A feature of this exhibit was the film of motion pictures showing the great *Turnfest* at Frankfort-on-the-Main, and also the last *Bundesturnfest*, held in Cincinnati. One of the many appeals to the "gesammten Deutschtum," showing in what inspiring words the exhortations to their national feeling were expressed, was as follows: "Es war die deutsche Turnerei, welche vor hundert Jahren den zerbröckelnden germanischen Stämmen neuen Halt und neue Lebenskraft verliehen hat. Es ist die deutsche Turnerei, die dem Deutschtum hier in Amerika eine Heimstätte zur Pflege deutscher Ideale geschaffen hat. Es sind die deutschen Turnerschaften von Denver, welche am 8. Mai im Auditorium einen neuen Geist heraufbeschwören wollen, damit unseren Deutschen Ehre und Achtung zuteil werde.—Das grosse Bundesturnfest pocht an die Tür; die Augen der Welt sind auf uns gerichtet."—April 27, 1912.

societies and many of the schools in the State. On the public schools, too, the *Turnvereine* have had a stimulating effect in that they have been influential in introducing and promoting systematic gymnastics in the schools. On Sunday, May 19, 1912, an imposing demonstration by 10,000 of the school children of Denver was given in City Park under the direction of the leaders of the three *Turnvereine,* Jacob Schmitt, Ernst Klaffe and Adolph Schmidt, assisted by Robert Schmitt, Robert Koch and a number of the public school teachers. Various gymnastic exercises, athletic games, drill and Maypole and aesthetic dances made an interesting program. The influence of the *Turnverein* is nowhere greater than on the children, who, however unconsciously, are receiving unaltered one of the best things the Germans have to offer. On the occasions of such public exhibits as was cited above, there is tremendous enthusiasm in the audience and a universal feeling that the German "Turners" are performing an inestimable service in Denver. A more subtle influence of these societies is that they stimulate a love for the German language. A young man whose parents were German, but whose training in the language of his fathers was very slight, confessed that it was with feelings of the deepest humility and regret that he observed his failing, when in attendance on the class exercises in the *Turnhalle.* It is customary with German parents, even with those who do not feel the importance of teaching their children German, to send them to the Turner halls to receive gymnastic instruction. In this way many receive the first real impetus to attain a proficiency in the German language.[1]

Again, in the theatre, Germans have exerted an influence on the social development of Colorado. Denver boasts a well

[1] The *Colorado Herold* says: "Die Deutschen im ganzen Lande — und besonders die Deutschen im Westen — haben eine hohe Kulturmission zu erfüllen, um einerseits den Beweis zu liefern, dass sie auf der Höhe der Zeit stehen und den Fortschritt auf erzieherischem Gebiet mit Thatkraft und Unternehmungsgeist zu würdigen wissen, andererseits den Amerikanern durch Veranschaulichung ihres besten Könnens und Wissens zu bezeugen, dass die nativistischen Angriffe, die allenthalben gegen die Ausländer gemacht werden, gänzlich aus der Luft gegriffen sind und der Wahrheit entbehren. Es ist deshalb Pflicht des gesammten Deutschtums, sich eine Ehre daraus zu machen . . . . fortwährend für die gute Sache einzulegen."—April 4, 1912.

managed German theatre where plays are produced in the German language, modern pieces that have been successful in Germany, as well as classical pieces. Like the *Turnverein*, the theatre exerts a manifold influence. It is a factor in the educational and cultural life and it stimulates public amusement.

Scores of German citizens in Colorado have ably followed professional careers, thus quietly aiding in the social betterment of the community. There have been many examples in the medical profession of Germans who have won marked distinction. Among them was William Harmon Buchtel,[1] whose father was a native of Stuttgart, and who for many years practiced medicine in Denver. He became well known both for his large practice and through his connection with various medical associations. David H. Coover,[2] likewise of German parentage, is another of Denver's distinguished medical scholars, also Oscar Joseph Pfeiffer, at one time visiting surgeon of St. Luke's hospital, T. J. Horn, who, by the way, was a lineal descendant of Martin Luther,[3] Louis Auerbach, J. Ernest Meien and John Elsner. In legislative and judicial lines, Germans have shown marked ability. Already in 1860, we find a German, Charles Dahler, serving as election judge. The Hon. Frederick J. Ebert was a member of the Constitutional Convention of 1876 and assisted in framing the fundamental law of the State. The Hon. Silas B. Hahn who was of German ancestry, was a member of the Colorado Territorial

[1] Dr. Buchtel has been associated with the State Medical, *Denver* and Arapahoe County and the American Medical Association, was a charter member of the Western Association of Obstetrics, was professor in the Gross Medical school and physician to St. Luke's Hospital.

[2] Dr. Coover held the position of clinical ophthalmology and otology in Gross Medical College; he was especially famed as specialist in diseases of the eye and ear. He was an active member of the American Association of Railway Surgeons, the American Medical Society, the Colorado State Medical Society, the Denver Pathological Society and the Denver and Arapahoe County Medical Society. Cf. *Denver and Vicinity*, pp. 297, 500.

[3] Cf. *History of the Arkansas Valley*, pp. 389-476, 207-208; *History of Denver*, p. 308; Hall, IV, p. 428.

Legislature of 1870.[1] Among the pioneer dentists of German blood in Denver, we mention especially R. H. Bohn and George B. Hartung. The sign, "Deutscher Zahnarzt" is now very familiar in Denver.

Robert S. Roeschlaub, a native of Munich, is the architect to whom Colorado owes many fine buildings. Two years after opening his office in Denver (1873), he was appointed architect to the School Board. Nearly all the school buildings are said to have been erected under his supervision. Critics grant him wider commendation than any other American architect for excellence in design and uniform superiority of construction.[2]

Scarcely any profession has figured more prominently in the development of Colorado than civil and mining engineering. The celebrated founder of the German Colony in the Wet Mountain Valley, Carl Wulsten, worked untiringly at this profession, becoming an authority in surveying, draughting, mapmaking and engineering. Another German, Max Boehmer, a native of Lüneburg, located in Colorado in pioneer days and, during the years 1879-1898, was consulting mining engineer at Leadville.[3] Frederick J. Ebert came to Denver in 1860 with an engineering corps to survey the Kansas Pacific Railroad. Two years later, he drafted the first map of the Territory and assisted in making the first land survey. In 1863 he was appointed city engineer of Denver. His surveys are said to

[1] The Hon. A. W. Rucker, while judge of the criminal court of Lake County, distinguished himself for his ability, and for the fairness with which he carried out his decisions. Cf. *History of the Arkansas Valley*, pp. 207-388. John Heisler, as member of the House of the General Assembly, 1892-'94, introduced several important bills, among them the bill to charge tuition to students from other States attending the State University. Cf. Hall, IV, 472. Hon. Simon Guggenheim, of German parentage, was United States Senator from Colorado, 1907-'13. E. P. Jacobson, a native Prussian, was for many years a leading lawyer in Denver.

[2] Cf. Hall, IV, 345, 551-552. *History of Denver*, pp. 561. Many public buildings in Colorado owe to Mr. Roeschlaub their origin, among them the State Normal School at Greeley, the State Institute for the Deaf, Mute and Blind at Colorado Springs, many of the buildings of Denver University and the Trinity Methodist Church of Denver.

[3] Cf. *Who's Who in America?*—1908-1909, p. 178.

be the only ones that have stood the test of time and of the law.[1]

The pages of Colorado's political history abound with examples of German citizens who, in office and out, have striven successfully for large and important issues. William H. Meyer and Frederick J. Ebert, as members of the Constitutional Convention, aided in the perfecting of Colorado's statehood. William N. Byers, another public-spirited German, labored incessantly for the admission of Colorado to the Union. A recent Governor of the State, the Hon. John F. Shafroth, a German of the second generation, had, before rising to the dignity of the gubernatorial chair, an excellent record in the practice of the law. While member of Congress (1894-1898), he introduced bills providing for the opening of forest reserves to exploration and to mining claims, and helped secure the passage of a bill providing for water reservoir sites at numerous points in Colorado and also providing for the protection of the forests from fire.[2] Hon. E. P. Jacobson, a Prussian by birth, while a member of the Colorado State Senate, introduced and vigorously championed a bill for railway regulation. Among the German pioneers of 1860 who were members of the legislature were Hans J. Kruse, a native of Holstein, Louis F. Bartels, of Hannover, and Judge Amos Steck, a German by descent.[3] As State Senator, Henry Suess, a native of Hesse-Cassel, filled well his position as chairman of the roads and bridges improvement committee of the legislature, 1885-1886. Likewise, in city and county offices, many German citizens have held important positions, as: John H. Behrens, a native German, mayor, city treasurer, etc., of Evans, Colorado; Edward Monash, born in Posen, President of the board of Public Works and Park Commissioner, Denver; Rudolph Koenig, mayor of Golden; Samuel Clammer, mayor of Fort Collins; John L. Herzinger, mayor of Loveland; also August

[1] Name originally Eberhart. Cf. *History of Denver*, pp. 416-418. *Denver and Vicinity*, p. 400; Hall, IV, p. 431.

[2] Cf. *Western Press Bureau*, 956 Gas & Electric Bldg., Denver. By permission of Gov. Shafroth.

[3] Cf. Hall, IV, pp. 485-486, 490. *History of Denver*, pp. 587-588.

L. Rohling, Joseph C. Cramer, Charles Seitz, Michael Dueber, Albert Walter and Joseph Schutz, who have held positions in city councils, etc.[1]

Summarizing the results found in the present chapter, it has been shown that the Germans in Colorado have, like their fellow countrymen everywhere in the United States, been active in religious organizations. They have established and supported a large number of German churches in proportion to their numbers, besides giving their support to many in which the English language is spoken. In addition to their religious work, the German churches exert a broadening influence on their environment and an educating influence on their attendants. As it is to Germany that the world has long looked with deep respect in matters pertaining to education, so it was to the Germans in Colorado that we looked with keen interest to learn what they have done for the intellectual life of the State. It has been shown in the foregoing pages that they have not been found wanting, but that they have been active in promoting the cause of education. German journalism in Colorado strives to inculcate the doctrine of the value of relaxation. By keeping this in mind, the German element performs a recog-

---

[1] County elections for the fall of 1864 had among the successful candidates the following: Arapahoe County, judge, H. J. Bredlinger, A. Hanauer, Samuel Brantner, William Hess, George C. Schleier; Gilpin County, Assessor, Frank Messenger; U. S. Assessor, Daniel Witter; Member of House of Representatives, Lake County, Jacob Ehrhart; Alderman, Tritch Kasserman. Cf. *Rocky Mountain News,* September 6, 1864.

The Territorial Government had the following German representatives:

1st Provisional Government—D. Shafer (of a council of 8).

3d Legislature 1864—Charles W. Walter, President, J. A. Koontz, H. Henson.

4th Legislature 1865—Hiram J. Brendlinger, J. H. Ehrhart.

5th Legislature 1866—Louis F. Bartels, T. C. Bergen, J. C. Ehrhart.

6th Legislature 1867—Jaocb E. Ehrhart, W. J. Kram.

7th Legislature 1868—Amos Steck, J. E. Wurtzbach, W. J. Kram, C. Leimer.

8th Legislature 1870—S. B. Hahn, Amos Steck, W. H. Meyer.

9th Legislature 1872—B. W. Wisebart, Frederick Steinhauer.

10th Legislature 1874—F. Steinhauer, J. H. Uhlhorn, W. H. Meyer, J. Koontz.

11th Legislature 1876—S. B. Hahn, Frederick Kruse, H. O. Rettberg, Herman Duhne.

nized service. By encouraging the people to relax they helped to produce a better balanced community, one possessing a keener zest for work and a capacity for greater accomplishment. We have seen the struggles of the attempts at a German newspaper in Colorado arrive at a happy conclusion. German societies, as we have noted, perpetuate the national customs for which, unfortunately, many of our immigrants find no adequate substitute in the new country. The *Turnvereine* stimulate interest in systematic exercise and in the intelligent care of the body. In arousing an interest in the German language, these societies influence, as well, the intellectual life of their members. Half a dozen professions, not including religious and educational fields, have been adorned by men of German blood in Colorado. They have, as pioneers, in several cases hewn their way through perplexing and disheartening conditions, they have promoted the cause in which they were especially interested, thus benefiting the entire community. Finally, in political life, we have seen many Germans filling important positions of trust. From the earliest days, they were conspicuous in advancing the cause of the Commonwealth, and their zeal has continued up to the present. The Germans in Colorado have never been office seekers; when the situation was calm, they were rarely heard in public affairs. It needed only the suggestion of a critical situation, however, to call forth their reserve of fighting strength for what they felt to be right and conducive to the best interests of the commonwealth.